IRA'S FARM

Why do farmers farm, given their economic adversities on top of the many frustrations and difficulties normal to farming? And always the answer is: "Love. They must do it for love." Farmers farm for the love of farming. They love to watch and nurture the growth of plants. They love to live in the presence of animals. They love to work outdoors. They love the weather, maybe even when it is making them miserable. They love to live where they work and to work where they live. If the scale of their farming is small enough, they like to work in the company of their children and with the help of their children. They love the measure of independence that farm life can still provide. I have an idea that a lot of farmers have gone to a lot of trouble merely to be self-employed to live at least a part of their lives without a boss.

—WENDELL BERRY,
BRINGING IT TO THE TABLE: ON FARMING AND FOOD

IRA'S FARM

GROWING UP ON A SELF-SUSTAINING FARM IN THE 1930'S AND 1940'S

Ira Mack, circa 1920

VIRGINIA JOHNSON

■

HARLAN VILLAGE PRESS 2018

IRA'S FARM

ISBN: 978-0-692-10031-8

First edition April 2018
0 9 8 7 6 5 4 3 2 1

Book design by Gail Dennis

HARLAN VILLAGE PRESS
virginiajohnson243@yahoo.com

TABLE OF CONTENTS

INTRODUCTION

Introduction

The day had been a good one. It was a warm, sunny October afternoon in Manistee as we left the annual get-together of nieces and nephews and in-laws from Saginaw, Bear Lake and points north. There's something special about sharing a turkey dinner and vintage photos and versions of events that only relatives can tell about each other. On the way back to Traverse City, I suggested to my daughter, Gail, and her husband that we drive past the farm where I grew up in Harlan. As we drew near the south field where my Dad, Ira, usually planted corn the sky had become overcast and the day a bit gloomy, as if to emphasize the now-desolated area. Brittle gray milkweed stalks and clumps of dried quack grass scattered here and there created a neglected, fallow impression of the field where once my younger brother, Gene, and I had helped harvest crops. Over across the pasture land, rusty barbed wire seemed to be the only thing holding up those weathered, leaning fence posts bordering the old potato field. Further on a few gnarly apple trees gave barely a hint of the once-flourishing fruit orchard that provided pears and plums and apples for the fresh juicy pies that came from a wood-stoked range oven. Only a row of maple trees with their autumn bouquet of red and orange and yellow leaves broke the somber appearance of the place I called home for twenty years. The sight of those maple trees brought thoughts of our family boiling down the spring-time sap until it thickened into mouth-watering syrup, ready to pour over a mound of hot pancakes.

A touch of melancholy welled up in me as we drove away. I recognized that I was as responsible for the neglected appearance of the farm as were other time-related circumstances. I didn't stay and mend the fences. I was one of those who abandoned the rusty old plow laying on its side in the far corner of the east field. I didn't keep the grapevines pruned or the garden cultivated. The times they were a-changin' my generation said as we headed for the city. The era of the small-time farmer was over, we said.

But we were wrong. Something innate within the human culture draws us like a magnet toward the soil, toward planting and nurturing and growing vegetables and feeding piglets and baby chicks or watching a new little calf stand up on its wobbly legs.

Small farms still struggle, still survive, still hold promise for the next generation.

A curious pleasure often fills me when I read of local events highlighting today's young farmers and the continuing growth of organic crops. I am amazed at the popularity of CSA's, of Small Farm Conferences, of elementary schools providing garden space and scheduling time to grow vegetables. In fact reading these articles provided me with the motivation for this book.

My dad's story of making a living on a northern Michigan farm in the 1930's and 1940's is an ordinary one. Dad was a quiet, unassuming person of slight build, just 5'7" and always slim. He dressed simply, preferred bib overalls. There's something about bib overalls that causes most males to swagger a bit as they walk, but my dad was not a man who ever displayed "swaggering" thoughts about any of his accomplishments. He always had his hair cut short, smoked a corn cob pipe, liked his coffee in the morning. He didn't smile a lot, but was a pleasant, soft-spoken person. Seldom argued, a bit reserved. At times it was downright difficult to engage him in a lengthy conversation, though he was friendly and liked having people around.

Perhaps his life and story are ordinary in one sense, yet a stream of stubborn hope and determination flow through those days, interspersed with bits of humor. Any journaling of his life is written from my memories, a few old letters and the stories my cousins and old neighbors tell. But each of us has a story to tell. We invent, explore, create, dream, stumble, start over. Alex Haley, author of the novel, *Roots*, once said, "Every time an old person dies, it's like a library burning down."

CHAPTER 1 (1896-1920)

EARLY LIFE OF MY PARENTS, IRA AND PAROLEE (VALENCOURT) MACK

≈❧

I love to learn about new words. I found one recently that may be the glue that holds this memoir together. The word "locavore" was featured in a recent issue of *Edible Grand Traverse* magazine. It is a noun describing a person who endeavors to eat only locally produced food and was awarded Word of the Year when first published in the 2007 *New Oxford American Dictionary*. I suppose the creation of a new noun occurs when a popular item or fad becomes common and needs a specific title. If that is how the term "locavore" came about, it is right on. Recent years have seen phenomenal growth in providing garden-fresh produce and local meat to restaurants and supermarkets and households.

In northwest Michigan, where I live, Community Supported Agriculture farms (CSA's) abound. Farmers' markets are crowded from May through October with shoppers looking for just-picked vegetables and fruits. Roadside stands overflow with right-off-the-vine produce along with jars of homemade jams and jellies, home-baked breads, cookies, and pies. Farm-to-table is the popular buzzword among proponents of the "buy local" movement.

In the 1930's, most foods on a rural supper table fit the term farm-to-table. When a farmer sat down to eat his meal of mashed potatoes and gravy, beef roast, green beans and apple pie, he could be sure that it was locally grown. It came from his garden, his fruit orchard and his "back forty" pasture. Wintertime, the family fare came from root cellars, Mason canning jars or an earthenware stone crock in the basement. Taproot veggies, such as parsnips and carrots, provided the ultimate in winter's fresh foods when dug from the garden after snow had blanketed the ground.

Outdoor root cellars, devised to store a variety of vegetables underground, were common on farms where winters were harsh and temperatures below freezing. An enterprising couple, Scott and Helen Nearing, who moved to a farm in Vermont during the Depression years of the thirties, relied greatly on root cellars for storage. In their 400-page book, *The Good Life*, they describe their attempts to build inexpensive, compact and convenient in-ground cellars, along with other novel storage units. The Nearings spent sixty years developing a self-sufficient lifestyle and compiled a treasure of hints for self-sustained living. They were models of true locavores long before the word was coined.

Perhaps a farmer like my dad, who worked a small sixty-acre farm, could be considered a locavorist since he provided locally-grown products for his family. (Note to lexicographers who search for the word "locavorist" in your favorite dictionary: it's not there. The word is simply one that seems to describe the suppliers, and so I claim writer's privilege for its usage.)

My dad's story began February 20, 1896. Ira, born to Milo and Ada (Groat) Mack, lived his entire childhood and early adult years on a farm near Marlette in southeastern Michigan. Not much is known about his boyhood; no humorous or hair-raising tales ever surfaced at family reunions. His mother, Ada, was a staunch Baptist, so I imagine the whole family spent Sunday mornings in church. Dad likely attended a one-room schoolhouse with a wood-stoked stove and outdoor toilet facilities. He may have walked to school. No information is available of how much education he received, though many in that era did not go beyond the eighth grade. Transportation was most likely by horse and carriage in the summer and a sleigh or cutter in the winter. (A cutter is smaller than a sleigh and designed with seats for more leisure travel.) Very few families could afford autos until Henry Ford's invention of assembly line auto production in 1914—an invention that made the Model T Ford affordable for the average family.

Grandpa Milo Mack had a huge, droopy mustache all of his adult life. He was an independent sort of man—never learned to drive a car, never owned one, never wanted one. I loved the stories of him perched atop a springboard seat on his horse-drawn wagon, riding into Marlette to peddle fresh vegetables from his garden. He was also an enterprising fellow—a sign in his front yard advertised "Saws Sharpened" and "Shoes Repaired." The oft-repeated adage, "If the shoe fits, wear it," may very well have originated from those years. Younger children in the family often inherited the outgrown shoes of their older siblings or a cousin. Many homes had their own shoe repair tools, such as awls, metal shoe forms, hammers and shoe tacks needed to replace worn soles or heels. Shoe cobbler shops could also be found in most towns.

Grandma Ada Mack, of Dutch heritage, was a descendant of Philip Grööt (later known as Philip Groat) who left his homeland in Rotterdam, Holland, in 1710 and settled on the banks of the Mohawk River near what is now known as Amsterdam, New York. History notes he was the first white man in the area to negotiate with the Mohawk Indians for a parcel of land. The deed to his property was described as "the land on the north bank of the Mohawk River between two creeks and as far north as the grantee desires." Later that winter, Philip hitched up his horse and cutter and journeyed up the frozen waterway to explore his new purchase, which he had not yet seen. On the way, his cutter broke through the ice and Philip drowned, never having set foot on the land between two creeks. His wife and three sons later settled there and built the first grist mill in the area.

Ira at Camp Custer, Battle Creek, Michigan, March 1918

Over the years, Grandma Mack, in addition to raising her family, gained a reputation as a neighborhood caregiver. If someone knocked on her door needing help with a baby birthing or had an illness in their home, Grandma invariably just asked for a minute to comb her hair and change her apron. She also served as a Red Cross volunteer and when the Great War erupted, a war later known as World War One, she joined the women who sewed bandages for our allies overseas.

As a nation, we were soon drawn into the war. Britain and France sent an urgent plea for weapons and troops. In February 1918 Dad received his draft notice and reported to Camp Custer near Battle Creek, Michigan, where he began training as an army medic. He was then assigned and shipped overseas to Camp Sussex Infirmary in La Pallice, a port city located on the Bay of Biscay in southern France. Settling into a military-disciplined life surrounded by French soldiers, battleships, army trucks and armed personnel, Dad must have wondered what planet he had landed on—certainly one bearing no resemblance to his home in rural Sanilac County. He served in Camp Sussex until his discharge the following year. Letters he wrote home bore the logo of the American Expeditionary Forces (AEF), the umbrella under which General John Pershing directed all U. S. military personnel serving overseas.

The Sussex hospital base was one of over two hundred infirmaries constructed by Allied forces as they focused on the need to provide faster and better care to soldiers. WWI is historically noted for being in the forefront of efforts to give more humane care for the wounded. Because of the overwhelming need for blood-transfusions, doctors working in the base camp hospitals developed a system to improve the availability of blood for immediate use. Though the first attempt to store this was a crude one by today's standards, it saved lives and ultimately led to the modern blood banks we now take for granted as an integral part of treatment. Prior to that, blood transfusions were a time-consuming process of locating a donor and then performing a direct transfer-ence from the donor to the wounded soldier. Dad would learn first-hand of the vital need for bandages and perhaps he remembered the many days his mother spent sewing bandages at the Red Cross building in Marlette.

Like many servicemen, Dad talked very little about his responsibilities as a medic. In a letter written to his sister, Flora, he mentioned attending a USO dance at a nearby Army base and going on an ambulance trip to Base Hospital #69 one hundred fifty miles away. In the same letter he said that he had been promoted to Private First Class, adding, "That is high enough for me. A fellow never has to worry over anything when he is a private. The sergeants and corporals catch all the blame."

But the tragic effects of war were no doubt evident all around him. First-time use of new military weapons such as mustard gas, military tanks, the infamous trench battle lines, and reconnaissance bi-planes which later became engaged in air battles and dropped crude bombs, brought horrors of war never before experienced. Orville Wright, of the Wright Brothers aviation fame, is reported to have said, "The aeroplane has made war so terrible that I do not believe any nation will care to start a war again."

Planes were not alone in causing devastation among the ranks. An epidemic of Spanish flu raged across Europe in the midst of the war, claiming the lives of thousands of military personnel in its wake. No vaccine was available to stop its rampant spread as it engulfed the world. Dad received word in December of 1918 that his brother, Berton, a public school teacher, married with three children, had succumbed to the devastating disease. Dad, of course, was unable to get home for his brother's funeral. Traveling from Europe to the United States at that time involved four or five days by ship. It would be yet another nine years before Charles Lindbergh flew the first transatlantic flight across the Atlantic Ocean in May of 1927. Lindbergh's flight would awaken the dream of future worldwide air travel.

The Great War ended with a truce signed November 18, 1918. It would be another seven months before Dad, along with hundreds of other homesick and war-weary soldiers, arrived on American soil aboard the USS *Housatonic*.

As a family, we respect and honor Dad's military service, but we are also aware that only Dad could tell us how his life was shaped by what he saw in those few years.

What he learned about war and nations and mankind. Was he a pacifist because he saw what violence can do to a person? Was he always a quiet introvert or did his wartime experiences cause him to dislike arguments and confrontations? Did his time overseas bring him new awareness of the value of home and family? We have no answers to these questions but certainly the man he became was influenced by the realities of war and its toll. A man slow to anger and quick to listen, he lived his life without pretense. A man with roots as deep as the crops in his fields.

My parents' love story began the following summer in Harbor Beach, Michigan, a popular Lake Huron resort area at that time. Dad rented a room in a local boardinghouse while looking for work. Boardinghouses accommodated single men, often returning servicemen, providing a place to live and three meals a day at nominal rates. Dad soon began dating the cook, a petite young woman with sparkling brown eyes named Parolee Valencourt. She would one day become my mother. Parolee (generally pronounced Par'lee, usually called by her nickname, Polly) lived in northern Michigan, but was in Harbor Beach for the summer to be near her sister, Bertha. We will never know for certain whether it was Mom or her scrumptious apple pies that Dad fell in love with, but by the end of summer they were making wedding plans. In September Mom was back in Harlan, a small town up north in Wexford County, to prepare for their October 27th wedding. A copy of their marriage license lists Flora Mack, Dad's younger sister, as Mom's bridesmaid, and Perry Valencourt, Mom's older brother, as Dad's best man, but little else is known about the wedding day. If there were any photos taken, they have since disappeared; not even a formal pose of the bride and groom has surfaced. But years later, we siblings were given an unexpected glimpse of their plans through a couple of letters Mom had written to Dad a month before their wedding. Fragile pages, kept by Dad for over half a century, revealed a hint of the excitement between our parents and their impending marriage.

Excerpts from the first letter written by Mom September 28, 1920, include: "My dear Ira, I'll bet this winter will be the happiest we have seen yet. I am looking forward to it. What are you going to do at our place before you come up or don't you want to tell? Hattie [a sister-in-law] wants to get acquainted with you if we stay over Sunday.

"My Love, I have your picture on my stand all the time so I can look at it every time I come into my room. You seem to be watching me tonight. Four weeks from tomorrow is our wedding day. We will have to have a table, cook stove (or oil stove) and some chairs before we live in that house unless we go without something to eat. Isn't that right, kiddo? Is there an orchard on the place?

"My Dear, I am going to have a white dress and white slippers and stockings. A navy blue suit will be alright. The minister in our church said in his sermon Sunday that a girl should not wear an engagement ring because it is an ornament. It is against the rules of our church to wear gold, but it is not against my religion. Love from your future wife, Parolee." The gold ring decision tells a lot about the independent nature of my mother.

In yet another letter she describes the crop of grain just harvested on the family homestead. She wrote, "The boys [her brothers] raised buckwheat, rye and wheat and reaped nearly fifteen hundred bushels of grain. Isn't that great?" Mom was definitely a farm girl.

The village of Harlan, located 30 miles south of Traverse City, where Mom was born and raised, is no longer even a dot on local maps. It was a hub of activity, however, in the early 1900's when Mom's parents, Henry and Leona (Northrup) Valencourt, were raising their family of eleven children—Fred, Perry, Lena, Herman, Parolee (my mom), Bertha, Lawrence, Joseph, Mike, Bessie and Mary. Situated on the county line road dividing Manistee and Wexford counties, the village boasted a general store, railroad depot, a small community church, ice house and sawmill. Plans were being drawn up for a new elementary school building. Farming was the main industry.

Grandpa Valencourt was an industrious farmer, eventually owning over one hundred acres of farm land. Six strong, husky sons no doubt contributed to his success. The homestead in which they raised their eleven children is still standing and most of the buildings are in good repair. The road by the house is still an unimproved, gravel-covered, little-traveled, short stretch of roadway.

At the time of Mom's birth in 1897, there were already three boys and one girl under nine years old in the Henry Valencourt household. By the time Mom reached seventeen years old, six more children had been added to the family. It's probably safe to assume Mom's early years were spent helping her mother amidst a boisterous and noisy household. It is family lore that all eleven children never sat down together to eat a meal. They did, however, have one family photo taken in later years with all of the siblings in it. Copies of this are still in the family archives.

The Cleon Township Cemetery on Faylor Road, a few miles from Harlan, contains a virtual geneaology of Valencourts. The old section contains the tombstone of Mom's paternal grandparents, Joseph Valencourt (1842-1901) and his wife, Virginia, born in 1843, but no date of her death. She moved to Multnomah, Oregon, after Joseph's death. Just a few steps away are the gravestones of Mom's maternal grandparents, Spafford Northrup (1828-1898) and his wife, Charity (1842-1918). Also nearby are the graves of Mom's parents, Henry (1863-1937) and Leona (Northrup) Valencourt (1867-1934). My parents are buried in the new section accross the road.

Mom started school in 1902 in a one-room schoolhouse along with twenty other students. A sister and three brothers were among that small group. With three brothers there, I suspect no little boy teased Mom or pulled her hair that year.

Memoirs from Glen Shelton, Mom's brother-in-law, related this story: "One Sunday in 1908, I went to Sunday School at the little Church of the Brethren in Harlan. Just after I was seated, two little girls came walking down the aisle followed by their two older brothers. The girls were dressed in white with wide sloppy-brimmed soft straw hats. They were Bertha Valencourt and her sister, Polly."

Mom was a long-time member of the Harlan Brethren Church. I often walked to Sunday School there as a young girl. A small, seldom-used cemetery still remains open along the country road leading to the maple grove where the church stood. The words "Harlan Brethren Cemetery" can be seen engraved on a leaning section of the gate.

When the new elementary school was opened in Harlan, Mom attended there, but I have no knowledge of how many years of schooling she finished. In 1919, she attended Ferris Institute (now Ferris State University) in Big Rapids for one year.

MARRIAGE, ROARING 20'S, PURCHASE OF FARM IN HARLAN

My parents began married life on a rented farm near Dad's family in the Marlette area. By the time their daughter, Marjorie Ardella, and son, Kenneth Dean, were born, the nation was awash in social changes. A country weary of war and still reeling from the calamitous flu epidemic ushered in an era of freedom and prosperity. Automobiles, including Henry Ford's Model T, were in great demand and brought plentiful employment opportunities, good wages and mobility. Passage of the 18th Amendment gave women the right to vote, thanks to the efforts of the Women's Suffrage Movement. My mother could now cast her first vote for a national president in the 1920 presidential election between candidates Republican Warren Harding and Democrat James Cox.

In addition to the women's right to vote, Congress passed a law prohibiting the production and sale of alcoholic beverages, attempting to curb the alarming growth of alcohol consumption and its resulting problems.

Daring young adult women, in defiance of the Prohibition Act, began to drink gin and whiskey, wear short skirts, bob their hair and smoke cigarettes. They became known as flappers. Young men cruised around in their shiny new open-topped autos, looking dapper with their hair slicked back. The Charleston dance was all the rage. Speakeasies, where illegal alcohol could be purchased, sprung up in cities. Bootleggers, involved in buying and selling illegal liquor, suddenly had lucrative businesses, albeit ones fraught with danger. Chicago, New York City, Los Angeles, and Paris became magnet cities for affluent young adults. A novel, *The Great Gatsby*, written by F. Scott Fitzgerald in 1925, provided an intimate glimpse of the era, a period which soon became known as The Roaring Twenties.

Though my mother and dad appeared untouched by the ongoing social upheaval, there were changes of a different sort occurring in their own life. In January 1925, Dad received this notice from the U.S. Veterans Bureau:

"Dear Sir: I have the honor to transmit to you herewith your Adjusted Service Certificate, issued pursuant to the World War Adjusted Compensation Act in the amount of $1,234.00, based upon the amount of your Adjusted Service Credit, as certified to this Bureau by the Department which you last served while in the Military or Naval forces of the United States. If correspondence be necessary with this Bureau in regard to your Adjusted Compensation, you are respectfully requested to refer to A1977981.

(Signed) For the Director, O. W. Clark, Chief of Adjusted Compensation Division. Certificate enclosed."

What a welcome letter for a young married couple to receive—probably enough to buy a car and fulfill Dad's dream of making a down-payment on a small farm. Model T's were selling for about $300. But to their disappointment, Congress never enacted the legislature to dole out the promised bonus. The Certificate of Service became just that—a paper certificate with no hope for remuneration.

They would soon experience a much deeper heart-breaking experience. Their daughter, Ina Rosalie, born in June of 1925, lived just a short forty days before pneumonia took her life. They held the funeral service for their baby in their home.

The Roaring Twenties era had shown no signs of abating by this time. With the Prohibition Act still being enforced, selling contraband liquor had led to much criminal activity. But the family entertainment world also was in the midst of a positive change, one ushering in the advent of film. Silent movies with stars such as Rudolph Valentino, Charlie Chaplin, Fatty Arbuckle and the Laurel and Hardy team fascinated the nation with a new genre of light-hearted humor. In 1929, Walt Disney's beloved Mickey Mouse was introduced to adoring fans, young and old alike. The movie cartoon, "Steamboat Willie," starring the big-eared mouse continued to sell out wherever shown. The Jazz Age ushered in the first talking picture film, *The Jazz Singer*, starring Al Jolson. Ernest Hemingway's first published novel, *The Sun Also Rises*, became a bestseller. Babe Ruth hit sixty home runs in the 1927 baseball season. Charles Lindbergh made his first trans-Atlantic solo flight. The tube radio became a regular fixture in most homes, along with a phonograph. Phonograph records were all the rage and millions were sold. The Prohibition Act was finally repealed in December 1933.

As far as the family knows, Mom never became a flapper and Dad did not slick back his hair over those ten years. Both remained "bib overalls and homemade aprons" kinds of people. Bib overalls and aprons would soon be the order of the day—they had found a farm to buy and, after signing on the dotted line, a sixty-acre farm in Harlan was theirs.

In just those ten short years from 1919-1929, Dad had been drafted into the armed services, shipped overseas to France, tended wounded soldiers, lost a brother to the flu epidemic, met the love of his life, married, had three children, experienced the loss of a baby daughter, lived through the Roaring Twenties and now owned property along the Manistee-Wexford county line on the road to Harlan. Their new mailing address was Route #2, Copemish, Michigan. At age thirty-two Ira had his farm.

CHAPTER 3 (1930-1936)

FARM, STOCK MARKET FAILURE, RECOVERY, VILLAGE OF HARLAN

❧

Delia Hotchkiss, the former owner of their new farm, was also my mother's aunt. A very astute landowner, her property would be termed "turnkey ready" in today's real estate jargon. It included a comfortable two-story wood frame house, large barn, a fruit-bearing orchard, a row of Concord grapevines, windmill, henhouse, cistern, and an outdoor privy. Thanks to Delia's foresight, mature maple, poplar and elm trees provided an umbrella of shade around the house. A thorny hedge stretched the length of the front yard. The hedge seemed of little value, but Delia may have thought it added a stately appearance to the property. It remained a thorn-infested sentinel and a bane to barefoot kids all the years we lived there. Four ten-acre plots of tillable land, threaded seamlessly together with barbed wire, created a patchwork quilt of crop-land bound by cedar fence posts.

Who could have predicted that just three months after Mom and Dad moved into their new home the nation's stock market crash would bring chaos to banks and other financial institutions? It was an event of such disastrous proportions that it would lead to a decade of panic—a period often called the Great Depression.

There had been no time for Dad to establish a viable farming operation before they began to feel the financial effects of the nation's troubles, but there seemed no choice but to continue working the land. For the first couple of winters he depended on eggs from the laying hens and milk from the small herd of cows, along with the fruit orchard and vegetable garden, to carry them through. Wood chopped and hauled from the back corner of the property, kept them warm. Marjorie and Dean kept the woodbox full. But times continued to get tougher. By 1933, tentacles from the havoc on Wall Street now entangled even the rural sections of the nation. Grain prices tumbled. Markets closed. My parents got behind in payments on the land contract. Stories circulated among local farmers of property being repossessed, of families standing in food lines to keep their children fed.

On March 4, 1933, Franklin Delano Roosevelt became the 32nd President of the United States. Immediately after his inauguration Roosevelt began a radio blitz to offer hope and encouragement to the American people. He challenged the nation to remember that the only thing we have to fear is fear itself. It became his mantra. Jobs programs became top priority. The Works Progress Administration (WPA) established a program to build and repair governmental infra-structures such as roads and bridges. A tentative spirit of optimism and hope began to stir among those who had lost so much.

By 1934, the Ira Mack family consisted of Marjorie and Dean in grade school, I was now a three-year-old, and Eugene, a toddler just learning to walk. It was about this time that my parents received a letter from Delia, one which provided the reason why Dad was able to keep the farm, though he was so far behind in payments. The letter was one they may have been expecting and perhaps dreading. Was Delia writing to tell them she needed to foreclose on their debts? Could it be possible that they might lose the farm? They must have realized their future could easily hang on the contents of the letter. There was no mistaking the meticulous handwriting on the envelope. Delia's penmanship still resembled the flowing Palmer Method of cursive writing taught in grade schools. And though most personal letters of that era were written with pencil, Delia used a fountain pen dipped in an inkwell, its occasional ink blob adding a touch of character to the neatly-composed missive.

Delia began her letter by inquiring about their health, telling of her need to get new false teeth, asking about her brother Henry (Mom's father), but then the numbers appeared: "Either you or I have made a mistake in our record-keeping. I show that the last payment you made in full on your interest was $17.50 on October 1, 1931 and since then you made four partial payments of $10, $6 and two for $7 each making a total of $30. The total interest due for the years 1932, 1933 and 1934 was $105, so you still owe $75 on the back interest according to my books. Would you check your records? Either you or I have made a mistake. Must close for now and get dinner ready. Love, Delia."

Not one word suggesting immediate payment, just making sure their records matched. Delia must have trusted that when there was money available, payments would be continued. Dad probably grabbed his bib overalls off the kitchen hook and headed for the barn, perhaps remembering FDR's admonition: The only thing to fear is fear itself.

Financial recovery began slowly in the farming communities. Dad could at least look forward to each new spring knowing there would be calves born, new little chickens hatched, and his sturdy team of horses would be raring to be hitched to a plow. He continued to milk cows, feed chickens and cut wood. It would take time to raise a productive cattle herd, to bring field equipment up-to-date and repair neglected machinery. Little profit could be made until crop prices edged upwards. Though the farm was his, he remained vulnerable to the nation's circumstances.

One asset of the farm location was the road we lived on. It was unpaved during those years, but graders and plows kept it passable and usually in very good condition, since it was the Wexford-Manistee County line road and therefore saw quite a bit of traffic. It was generally the first road in the immediate area to be plowed after a snowstorm. Lined with maple and elm trees and a number of well-built, well-kept homes, it led to the village of Harlan, about two miles north. The larger towns of Cadillac, Manistee and Traverse City were each about thirty miles away.

Another welcome asset was the Wagner's General Store in Harlan with kegs of nails, gloves, jack-knives and all sorts of small items that saved farmers from making a trip to a larger town. Mr. Wagner sold gasoline, before electricity, when the clear glass cylinder atop a high base held the fuel, an attendant lowered the spout attached to a hose into the car's gas tank and the gasoline was gravity-fed from the glass container above. Only the clerk could service those fill-ups—no self-serve. Gasoline brands such as Sinclair, with their green dinosaur logo, and Mobil's flying red horse were seen at most small country stores. Wagner's store often became a gathering place for men to stand around and talk about their farms, or their cattle—or their women. By the mid-1930's the Wagner General Store stocked groceries, dry goods and kept ice in a nearby building to provide ice for kitchen ice boxes during the summer months. Sawdust and straw served as insulation to keep the ice frozen after it was cut from the Manistee River during the winter.

The Harlan Graded School just north of the village provided yet another primary asset to the local population. The cement block building, erected in 1911, was a result of a massive governmental effort to replace one-room schools and provide more and better educational facilities in rural areas. It included two main classrooms, a large all-purpose room, a basement with a small kitchen, a furnace and separate chemical toilet facilities for boys and for girls. Each bathroom included a sink, a pail of water to use for washing your hands and a large bucket under the sink to catch the wash water. Most of the students attending school there still had only outdoor toilet facilities at home and appreciated this modern convenience.

The daily run of the Ann Arbor railroad as it passed directly through the business area of Harlan served needs of the farmers, as well. Mr. Wagner managed the railroad depot, selling tickets, managing freight shipments in addition to his business as the general store owner. Harlan was one of sixty-six depot stops made by the Ann Arbor Railroad passenger train from Toledo, Ohio to Frankfort, Michigan. This rail service was a welcome convenience for local residents, including the twenty or thirty homes clustered near the store during those years.

A note about Harlan in later years: Ernest and Clara Dawkins lived just north of what used to be downtown

Harlan. The Dawkins family gave Harlan its moment of fame in later years. Clara and Ernest were grandparents of Pete Dawkins, the football player who won the Heisman Trophy in 1958. He went on to become a West Point cadet, a Rhodes scholar and a brigadier general in the U.S. Army. When Pete was a teenager, he spent a number of summers with his grandparents and in later articles about his life he described his visits as a time when he "learned to milk cows, help plant fields and slop pigs" and credited the experience as a bedrock in his life for learning self-reliance and hard work. He referred to Mrs. Dawkins as his "wonderful cigar-smokin' Grandma Clara."

Harlan School where my siblings and I attended grades K-8

CHAPTER 4 (1936-1940)

FAMILY STORIES, MONOPOLY, BEAN SORTER, 1939 WORLD'S FAIR

৵ঐ

Mom sold crates of eggs to the E. M. Wagner General store for resale whenever the hens were laying productively, providing a small cash flow. Farm eggs sold for twenty-one to twenty-six cents per dozen in 1935-36. All eggs coming from our farm could have been labeled "Cage free, farm fresh, vegetarian fed hens" similar to the description of many organic eggs now on the market. Our "free range" hens roamed the barnyard, the front yard and the ditch by the road, pecking and scratching for bits to eat. We scattered a little grain near the henhouse in the mornings and emptied vegetable peelings outside for chicken food. When warm weather arrived in the spring, we would usually see a mother hen emerge from the lilac bush in the front yard with six or seven new yellow chicks following close behind her. She hid the nest so well in the circle of new sapling bushes that we were not aware of it until she paraded past us with her brood. In another year the chicks would be pullets beginning to lay eggs, adding to our chicken count.

Perhaps Mom's egg money was what I held in my hands when I was allowed to go to the store with her. Some of my happiest memories as a little girl were when Mom or Dad took me to the store with them. So much candy, so few pennies—Mary Jane peanut butter chews, candy hearts, taffy, gum, and always those Tootsie Pop suckers all tightly wrapped in brown, orange, purple, yellow or red paper. The whole store fascinated me. I liked the sound of the creaking wood floors when we walked across them and the slamming of the screen door when customers entered or left. The meat case displayed rings of bologna and large round chunks of cheese. I wished Mom would buy a loaf of the store-bought, already-sliced Wonder Bread for our school lunch bag.

Whenever Mom added baking soda to her grocery list, I knew I would soon have one more bird card for my prized collection. Each bright orange Arm & Hammer Baking Soda box with its muscled-arm logo included a new card packed inside. The two-inch by three-inch card, wrapped in a cellophane envelope, featured a colorful painting of a bird on one side and some information about it on the other side. The "Useful Birds of America" series was published from 1908-1938 and its motto read: "For the good of all, do not destroy the birds." Artists Mary Eaton and Louis Agassiz Fuertes provided sketches of each bird in the series.

"Useful Birds of America" cards

The cards brought me an awareness of the species that were right in our yard.

I learned to identify them. One in particular, a Baltimore oriole, caught my attention when it made its nest in the tall poplar tree right near our kitchen door. That tree was huge, the trunk's circumference so large that it took two men to reach around it. Gnarly roots spread out around its base. Every autumn when the leaves had dropped from its branches we would see, high in the tallest part of the tree, an oriole's basket-like nest hanging near the tip of a drooping branch. It looked like it could easily break off and fall. I wondered then, and still do, how the young orioles learned to fly as they clung to such tiny branches that seemed always to be blowing in the wind. I remember the oriole's warble, a pleasant trill so easy to identify. I still have some of the Arm & Hammer bird cards though they were discontinued long ago and I never tire of seeing those tiny songbirds flitting in nearby bushes.

The years from 1933 to 1940 were the only years our whole family lived in the same house together, since Marjorie was twelve years old when Gene was born. Those were good years. We ate many meals together, spent evenings together, played games, took family photos, interacted with neighbors and our many Valencourt cousins, aunts and uncles.

My excitement one early September day in 1936 had very little, if anything, to do with Ira's farm or Mom's egg sales. I was on my way to the first day of kindergarten with a new dress on and shiny new shoes. The shoes felt kind of tight on my feet after being barefoot all summer, but they were new and black and beautiful. I walked through the door of that schoolhouse in wonderment—it looked so big—and was assigned to a little table alongside my best friend and cousin, Alvina. Together, over the next few years, she and I would learn to read the Dick and Jane Primer, print the alphabet in small and capital letters, conquer the Palmer Method of cursive writing (that beautiful style in which Aunt Delia's letter was written and a style that my sister, Marjorie, has retained all of her life), take our turn along with other students to solve arithmetic problems on the chalk blackboard, play on the trapeze, swing and teeter-totter (seesaw) at recess time. It was a heady time for two little girls who lived near each other and had played together almost from the time we learned to walk. We would be part of a community, a community of peers who would share a classroom in the Harlan school for the next eight years. As students, we gave recitations at PTA meetings and sang Christmas carols at school Christmas parties. All felt welcomed into the extended community. It seemed that we were greeted more warmly by adults when seeing them at a program or at the store. Perhaps it only felt that way because we were wiser now, having learned the alphabet and new songs and discovered new friends. A classmate, Maxine, was the daughter of Mr. Wagner, the store owner, and I envied her a bit, imagining that she could go out into the store anytime and get a piece of candy, a different hair ribbon or a new lined writing tablet.

One of very few traditions observed in our home was the annual New Year's Eve party when Uncle Mike, Mom's youngest brother, came to play cards and enjoy Mom's oyster soup, the only occasion that I remember her having oysters in the house. Uncle Mike was Alvina's dad, the cousin with whom I started kindergarten. He brought some new excitement that winter evening of December 31, 1936. In the past, after the traditional meal of Mom's homemade oyster soup, the family played cards, but this year Uncle Mike surprised everyone with the newest game on the market, a real estate game called Monopoly. How much fun that must have been for adults to buy property and houses and hotels, rolling out $1, $10 even $100 bills after years of pinching every penny to make ends meet. It was only paper money, but game players would spend countless hours jostling for deeds to property such as Park Place or Boardwalk, the pricey elite squares. Mediterranean and Baltic Avenues were the lowest cost to purchase, but also paid the least rent when a player landed on them. A roll of the dice could land you in "Jail". The original version, produced before plastics, included metal miniature objects in the shape of a shoe, a flatiron, top hat, dog and thimble to use for navigating around the board. The tiny red houses and hotels were built from genuine wood. Today, over eighty years later, Monopoly still occupies a place on the shelves of most toy shops and department stores, but the game pieces and houses are now made of plastic. (I recently found a metal flatiron Monopoly piece at a thrift shop and added it to my what-not collection.)

New Year's Eve was over. January 1937 had begun. Dad, now forty years old, with three seasons of planting and harvesting behind him since the Great Depression, was gaining confidence in his ability to continue farming. Neighbors and nearby grain elevators and livestock auction barns and pickle stations all contributed to a stellar group of assets in the agricultural community. Marjorie and Dean were old enough to help with housework and chores. With four growing children in the family, the pace of daily living on the Mack farm seemed always to be busy with things to do and places to go.

A newer and more dependable car became necessary and Dad began talking deals with McClish Auto Sales in Mesick. A 1928 Chevrolet Sedan suited his needs and it came time to sign a contract. But since cash was still not very plentiful and little equity had been built up on the farm property, collateral on the loan proved to be a problem. Dad and Mr. McClish solved the dilemma with the following contract: "… I do hereby sell and mortgage unto the said bank the following property free of encumbrances, and now in my possession in the township of Wexford, County of Wexford and State of Michigan to wit: one Guernsey cow 5 years old; one Holstein cow three years old, weight about 1,000 pounds; one Guernsey cow six years old and one black Jersey cow five years old." Dad must have trusted those mortgaged cows to keep producing, and they did. The loan was paid off on time.

Marjorie and I took piano lessons from the time we each were eight years old until near our high school graduations, but otherwise we were not a very musically inclined family. I never heard my Dad or my brothers sing. The wooden, twirling piano stool was used for seating guests as often as for piano players. Nor did any of the family have an artistic bent. I don't ever remember our family attending the theatre or a concert or stage play together, except the amateur ones in school. Mom went with friends to Manistee when *Gone with the Wind* first appeared and I saw *Snow White and the Seven Dwarfs* when it came to local theaters.

My brother, Dean, was a member of the Mesick Boy Scout Troop #42 the year they planned on taking a school bus to the 1939 World's Fair being held in New York City. Though money was still scarce my parents reasoned that this might be his only chance to see New York, so the whole family worked together sorting and bagging navy beans from last year's crop to sell for Dean's travel money. To accomplish this, the manual bean sorter was hauled down from the attic. The sorter was a simple, crude, wooden piece of equipment that operated on the principle of an assembly-line conveyor belt. When the beans which needed sorting were poured into the wooden hopper, a person sat at the canvas cloth conveyor belt and began pumping the pedals, resembling organ pedals, with their feet. As the beans fell down onto the belt the operator hand-sorted and discarded beans that were blemished, as well as little pebbles and dried bits of pod. It was tedious work, but kind of fun, as I remember. It became truly a family project to get those beans sorted and sold so Dean could have this "once-in-a-lifetime" experience to travel far from home. Little did we know that in a few short years he would join the Navy and sail to other countries like Greenland and Brazil and Japan.

The 1939 World's Fair theme, World of Tomorrow, introduced a brand of toothbrushes as one of the first everyday household items to contain a plastic formula. The Age of Plastics had arrived. Nylon stockings appeared in stores in 1940 and became the rage immediately. A department store in Connecticut sold their supply of four thousand pairs of stockings in the first three hours of business. The military began implementation of nylon in the production of parachutes, parachute cords, tents and other equipment. Within a few years, glass bottles were being replaced with plastic containers. Styrofoam cups appeared in restaurants and the uses for this new, unbreakable, lightweight material burgeoned. When synthetics appeared in fabrics, women loved the easy care of their dresses. Advertisements touted the new clothes, such as this one: "If it's nylon, it's prettier and oh! How fast it dries!"

CHAPTER 5 (1940-1945)

GENERAL HOUSEWORK DESCRIBED

The years leading up to the decade of the Forties were busy and productive times for my parents, but those same years seem etched in my mind as one continuous outdoor scene for my younger brother, Gene, and me. It was a world of play, of make-believe in a playground with no walls or boundary fences, with leaves and kittens and a rope swing fastened to a tree—a place where dirt and grass tickled our bare feet at every step, where we built forts and imaginary trails. That period in my life now seems almost to have an identity of its own, tangible in the formation of my values and the direction my life would take. It was a time of being taught without a teacher, just an acceptance time of life gifting my days in ways I could not discern at that young age.

When Marjorie left for business school, I was nine years old and began to help Mom in the kitchen. I soon understood that when Mom asked me to help, she expected me to finish my work, not just drop the task and run off to play. In retrospect I was being drawn into the daily routine of the art of farming, the ethics of family togetherness, learning to give and take.

Much of my mother's work revolved around the kitchen area, since the kitchen seemed to serve as kind of a hub for daily activities for everyone. It was a pleasant room, catching the morning sun through an east window, and the entry door facing south had a large window where the sun streamed through most of the day. Many visitors never got beyond the kitchen area, especially if it was time for a cup of coffee. Entering via the kitchen meant opening a wooden screen door with the stretchy metal coil attached, a coil wound tightly which pulled the door shut and scraped many an ankle that didn't step in fast enough. Summer days on a farm attracts flies and some usually buzzed through the open door, also. An unsightly fly ribbon hung from the kitchen ceiling during hot weather. It would unwind slowly, stretch downward and catch those pesky insects on its sticky residue. In addition, we used a wire mesh fly swatter, especially during canning season. Sweaters and jackets hung on a hook in the kitchen, since the entryway had no mud room or closet. Wintertime, with heavy coats hanging on the hooks, boots piled beneath them and gloves and mittens tossed on the nearby counter, created a messy area in the kitchen.

If you were the fire builder on a cold winter morning, it was a good thing if you knew how to use kindling effectively and if you knew which wood burned the best and what size to put in the first layer of your fire. It does not take very long to learn this because if your fire doesn't light the first time, you will shiver in the cold room until the wood does begin to blaze with heat. The iron range in our kitchen was a wonderful, though somewhat monstrous, stove that performed multiple tasks when there was a good blaze in the tinder box. Those tasks included serving as a water heater, baking oven, room heater, cook stove, dryer for wet mittens and dish towels and whatever else needed warming or drying. It also took practice and skill to keep the baking oven at the temperature you needed when baking since there were no manual controls on the temperature gauge—it rose as the fire burned hotter, or cooled as the fire waned.

The built-in kitchen cupboards served as a wall between the kitchen and dining room, a convenient feature which meant many of the cupboards could be opened from the dining room area as well as the kitchen. Our wooden kitchen table was about the size of a large desk top and always covered with a bright flowered oilcloth. It served as a work space as well as our main common meal table, and sometimes it became a "catch-all" which we had to clear off when it was time to set the table for a meal. We seldom ate at the round oak table in the dining room except when we had company. That larger dining table usually held a half-finished jigsaw puzzle and some books and magazines.

Our kitchen sink had a small pitcher pump attached that we used to draw water up from the cistern. This particular cement cistern, built before my parents purchased the farm, was quite a large underground vat adjacent to the kitchen area. Eaves troughs attached to the lower edge of the house roof caught the rain, draining it into the cistern. Rain water had a much softer quality than water from our well. The sink—a large, shallow rectangular cast-iron model—had a towel bar attached at one end, a mirrored medicine cabinet on the wall above it and a curtain surrounding the space underneath. A small basin kept in the sink served for washing our hands and face. Since it was the only sink in our house, we also washed our hair, brushed our teeth, and Dad shaved his whiskers there. He kept his leather "strop" hanging on a hook nearby. Stropping his straight razor aligned the fine steel of the six-inch razor for ease in shaving his face. It seemed like we used our sink for cosmetic reasons more than peeling vegetables or cleaning pots and pans. That was where we had easy access to water, and it naturally became the most convenient location.

A shelf adjacent to the cistern pitcher pump held a ten-quart galvanized pail for drinking water which we pumped from the outdoor well. It was not easy to keep cold water in the pail during the hot months of summer. The blue enamel dipper in the pail was used by everyone for getting a drink of water. After drinking from the dipper, it was put back in the pail. Separate drinking glasses for each person were not considered necessary. I have asked a number of people of my generation if that was their experience also, and the answer generally was "Yes, can you believe we really did that?" Often they added the comment "and we're still alive." But none of those questioned expressed a desire to return to the communal dipper.

Dishwashing in an aluminum dishpan on the kitchen table did not keep the water warm very long, so we kept a teakettle of hot water handy on the stove for re-heating the dishwater. Even the popular new Fels Naptha soap flakes lost their suds as the water cooled. By the time we finished washing the glasses and plates, it was hard to get grease off the cooking pans.

Cranking the butter churn in the kitchen was quite a pleasant chore; a girl could dream while turning cream into butter. The wooden churn had a little glass window that turned bluish and watery when the butter ball had formed. We emptied the remaining buttermilk out in the pig trough.

In the backroom just off the kitchen was the milk separator we used every morning and night when the milk pails were brought in. After reserving milk to use for drinking, the rest was poured into the steel bowl atop the separator. There was no pasteurization of the milk, but it was always taken care of immediately after milking the cows. Dad manually turned the crank handle and this allowed the disks, nested tightly together, to separate the cream from the milk. A stream of rich, thick cream would flow from one spigot while the skim milk

Mom never wanted a gas-powered washer, too noisy too smelly. (Ad from a 1930's farm magazine)

came down another. The disks were difficult to clean, but it was necessary that they be absolutely clear of any residue before the next use, so each morning and night they were washed in a pan of very hot water after finishing separating the milk and cream. The separator was set up in the same backroom where the butter churn, the laundry, the skeletal-like wood wringer and other items were stored, a room which should have been called an oversized junk drawer.

Behind a curtain along one wall of that room was the cardboard laundry box, usually filled with dirty socks and shirts and blue jeans that had been worn in the fields on dusty, hot days. Laundry day happened when the dirty clothes box overflowed, or when the day was sunny with a nice breeze to dry the clothes out on the line, or when everyone was around to help. All these factors eased the task of washday, which could be long and tiring. The galvanized tubs were set up in the same room as the separator. Dad poured a copper boiler of water, drawn from the cistern and heated on the stove, into the wash tub. The rinse tubs were filled with warm cistern water and set on the wood frame attached to a hand wringer. Mom scrubbed each soaked garment on a scrub board, squeezed the soapy water from it and dropped it into the first rinse tub. Whoever was helping her that day would swish the clothes up and down and guide them one at a time through the wringer while another person cranked the wringer handle. After rinsing them in the second tub, the clothes would be put back through the wringer the opposite way, caught and put in a basket ready to be hung on the outdoor clothesline. On warm summer days, hanging the clothes up was a pleasant task, but if the day was cold and windy, your fingers could hardly hold on to the clothespins. It was a most welcome time when we finally had an electric washing machine in the house and could throw the old scrub board away. However, an electric dryer was never considered a necessity and the clothesline remained out in the backyard for as long as my parents lived there. Clothes that were hung out on the line and dried in the fresh air brought a delightful and refreshing summer-day fragrance into the house. Perhaps that is the reason my mother never wanted a dryer after we had electricity.

Ironing day was next. The ironing board was set up in the kitchen because we heated two flatirons simultaneously on the stove, and with a detachable iron handle alternated the irons, keeping one always warming. The first step, strangely, was to lightly re-wet those recently dried clothes, either by dipping your fingers in water and sprinkling over the fabric, or in Mom's case, using an empty catsup bottle capped with a metal sprinkler head. The sprinkled garment was then rolled into a tight ball and put back in the same clothes basket which just hours ago had carried them in perfectly dry. Then we allowed an hour or two before ironing so that the clothes were damp enough for the iron to remove most of the wrinkles, since no cotton fabric could claim to be wrinkle-free at that time. Synthetic fabrics in clothing had not been developed, or at least, were not available in our household.

Always there was canning to be done in the harvest season. This often proved to be a challenge in July and August when sweltering weather arrived. We had to keep a fire in the kitchen range hot enough to boil water in the canner for twenty minutes. Mom was meticulous about clean, sterilized jars and only unblemished fruits could be used. We saved lids, canning jars, and rubber rims from year to year and tried always to avoid chipping the jar rims. They would be unusable if there was a crack or chip in the rim area. Glass jars that had no seal-tight lids were saved for jams and jellies because they could be preserved by sealing with hot wax.

Orchard owners, especially peach growers, often did their own marketing, peddling their ripe fruits door to door. Mom usually bought two or three bushels of freestone Red Haven peaches from them and we would be busy canning for a couple of days. At summer's end, our cellar shelves were filled with quarts of tomatoes, green beans, sweet corn, dill pickles, peaches, pears, apple sauce, wild blueberries and blackberries.

CHAPTER 6 (1941-1943)

WW2 Begins, Winter Blues

In August of 1941, just twenty-three years after WWI— the war which many believed to be the war to end all wars—America declared war on Germany. World War II had erupted in Europe, as it had in WWI, and American troops were deployed. Then on December 7, 1941 came the catastrophic attack on Pearl Harbor in the Hawaiian Islands and we were at war with Japan, as well. America suffered a grievous loss of servicemen as Japan's air fleet strafed U. S. Navy ships stationed there. This was no longer a distant war on foreign soil; a territory of the United States had been bombed. These conflicts ushered in a watershed era for me, for my friends, and for the generation we represented, though we were quite young. It was as if a world that we had so casually taken for granted came crashing into our carefree daily lives. It sobered us. We grappled with a new awareness of the world we lived in and came face to face with the thought that there were forces in the world that not only hated our nation, but could threaten our very freedom—a freedom that suddenly had become a fragile thing.

In subtle ways, and some not so subtle, the war began to invade every facet of daily living for most Americans. A number of 1942 Mesick High School graduates, including my brother Dean, planned to enlist in the service after receiving their diplomas. The war was on their minds constantly and even their baccalaureate invitations featured a soldier figure with a bright blue "V" for Victory on the cover. The battlefront news flooded national and local newspapers. Monthly issues of farm magazines began immediately to counsel farmers in ways they could assist in the war effort and to warn of impending shortages, such as gasoline and tires. The mood of the country shifted into one of patriotism and concern for our nation.

Dean enlisted in the Navy in December of 1942 and was stationed at Great Lakes Naval Station in Chicago. As with many homes at that time, we soon had a service flag hanging in a window facing the road. The white satin flag, about ten inches wide and fourteen inches long, had one blue star sewn on it, indicating one family member was serving in the military. Sadly, some families soon had gold stars on their flag, indicating a member of their family had become a casualty of the war. Dean was granted leave a couple of times that first winter. He easily found rides with other servicemen from his base as far as southern Michigan, but had to hitchhike the rest of the way home. It was a time in the nation when passing motorists almost always picked up a serviceman who had his thumb out needing a ride.

Even the popular outdoor free shows (pre-television) held in many communities on Saturday evening now featured a brief wartime newsreel by reporters such as Ernie Pyle. The newsreels were often garbled and out-of-focus yet the viewers, especially those with sons or daughters in uniform, welcomed any news and photos. The closest village where our family could enjoy the free movies was Mesick, about seven miles away, and was a weekly destination of entertainment for us. Mesick's "outdoor theatre" was located in an empty lot near the main shopping area. Movie-goers faced the large white film screen as they sat on rough, weathered wooden benches with no backrest. Show time began at dusk with a short serial film, usually a cowboy western, sometimes starring the Lone Ranger and Tonto. The serial always stopped with a cliffhanger scene designed to bring the viewer back the next week. Before and after the feature movie, women shopped and men stood on street corners gabbing while teenage girls walked around and around the downtown block checking out the guys, especially the guys with cars. It was Saturday Night Live in Mesick.

The winter of 1942-1943 seemed long and miserable to me, in a personal sense. I was eleven and a half years old. Marjorie worked in Traverse City and Dean was in the Navy. The house was now very quiet most of the time. And, perhaps because I was approaching those teen years with all their drama and mood swings, I began to realize the hardships of our farm life. For the first time, I sensed that we were a family without much extra money. I even felt embarrassed to ride in the family car because I thought it was so ugly. We still had no electricity. My bedroom was always cold. I remember this distinctly because after stormy nights there would often be snow on my windowsill. Looking back, I wonder why we didn't somehow fill in the cracks where snow had blown through. Not a priority, I guess. The only heat came from a floor register that allowed some warmth to filter up from the stove downstairs. Those wood-burning pot-bellied stoves which artists love to portray in paintings of the "good ol' days" were far from adequate for warming the house. The following winter Dad installed a new Heatrola, which forced out a more even heat into the room and could burn lumps of coal through the night. And the kerosene lamps displayed in antique stores to spark nostalgic memories, provided stringent lighting if you moved away from the arc of light it cast. Smoky lamp chimneys from the burning wicks were not easy to clean because they were fragile and easily broken, but they had to be washed in warm soapy water most evenings in the winter, along with trimming the wicks.

Vaccines for measles and mumps were not developed until the 1960's, and those diseases, plus scarlet fever, invaded most homes with growing children. I remember the bright red quarantine signs taped to the front of an entry door when scarlet fever had infected homes. If we were sick with a cold or fever, it was treated with Vicks or steam vapors or poultices. Mom must have learned of the medicinal qualities found in the catnip weeds in our yard—as kids, our chests were often plastered with a poultice using catnip leaves. A very interesting and informative book, *Just Weeds: History, Myths and Uses*, was compiled by Pamela Jones, a professional landscaper in the 1950's. She describes in great detail the characteristics of thirty common weeds, such as chicory and yarrow, and their culinary value and healing traits.

One of the least enjoyable aspects of winter before we had running water in the house involved white enamel chamber pots kept in each bedroom, complete with lid and a handle. Though it served as an alternative to wading through snow to the outdoor privy at night, it was the bane of my life until we had electricity and a flush toilet. And I still cringe at the memory of the discarded Montgomery Ward catalog being used for bathroom tissue. Using catalogs for bathroom tissue took the art of recycling way beyond necessary!

Baths consisted of a large, round galvanized tub, filled with warm water, and placed near the stove in the living-room. Needless to say, we did not get a daily shower. Even something as simple as a drink of cold water often meant putting on coat, boots, and mittens to go out to the pump and fill the empty water bucket. And when we needed a jar of canned food or potatoes for supper, it was necessary to go outside, walk the length of the porch, facing the wind and blowing snow, to get to the cellar door. My young impatient mind wondered why anyone would plan a cellar without an inside entrance. Apples were stored in baskets down there and potatoes were piled on a part of the floor with no cement, just dirt, which kept them cool enough to use fresh most of the winter. In later years Dean told us that he used to go down to the cellar sometimes and get a cold pork chop to eat. Mom had fried the chops, placed them in layers in a crock and covered each layer with hot lard as a preservative. Dean just wiped the lard off and ate that cold chop.

Laundry days in the winter generally meant wet clothes hanging all over the house, draped on a wooden rack or over the upstairs banister or on a hanger in the laundry room. If the sun was shining, a few items were hung on the clothesline. Dad's long underwear with the frozen back flap was a comical sight when first brought back into the house, not completely dried and still a little stiff.

Even the fresh-cut green fir Dad and Gene selected from our back woodlot for our Christmas tree that year seemed so scraggly and prickly-needled, I grumbled about its puny look. After it was decorated with colored construction-paper chains, tinsel, and some homemade ornaments, it did look a bit better. The clean pine fragrance that permeated throughout the house was nice, too. Marjorie came home with gifts for all of us, and the wrapped presents under the tree worked their magic—my discontent vanished into thin air.

In January we hung the new 1943 calendar on our kitchen wall. Each year the prominent black-lettered advertisement at the top remained the same—E. M. Wagner's General Store, Harlan, Michigan.

Mom became a Harlan news reporter for the *Cadillac Evening News*, receiving a free subscription as payment. Delivered by our mailman, it would keep our family informed about the war. Since very little criminal activity occurred in the village of Harlan (most likely zero disturbances), Mom's news reports usually consisted of events such as these from a 1942 column: "Ladies Aid will meet with Mrs. Les Rice on Thursday" or "Mrs. Fred Valencourt and daughter Bertha went to Kaleva for dental work Tuesday" or "Cleo Taylor and Byron Myers have been hauling ice for E. M Wagner."

January is usually a stormy month in Michigan and the winter of 1943 was no exception. Snow banks, when the plows finally cleared the road, were as high as the crossbars of the telephone poles, though I believe the telephone poles were shorter than those standing today. (In fact, they were short enough for mischievous boys with BB guns to shatter the glass insulators atop each crossbar—which did not please the local telephone company.) Harlan Road was often blocked for days at a time. One morning we had just finished breakfast when we heard a knock at the door. Who would be traveling on such a blustery day? It was the Farmer Peet salesman on his way to Wagner's Store. One bank of snow had drifted so high that he couldn't make his way through. Dad was quick to get his winter jacket and boots on, harness up the horses and walk with him back to the truck. The farmer's kind of horsepower had him out without a problem. When Dad got back home, he had a little grin on his face. We could hardly believe our eyes when he held up two big rings of bologna.

Winter was also a time to order needed items for the next year from the Montgomery Ward or Sears & Roebuck catalog, as the spring issue came in the mail while we were still shoveling snow banks. The self-addressed envelope tucked in each issue gave the Chicago address as simply Montgomery Ward, Chicago, Illinois. No street name or box number needed, just lick-and-stick a three-cent stamp on it. (Self-adhesive postage stamps came on the market in 1974.) My parents found it more convenient to send an order in the mail than to make a trip to the Ward's store in Traverse City.

Saturday nights of most winters, and this winter was no exception even with the war always on the minds of most people, also brought fun and entertainment at the Pomona Grange Hall where neighbors played cards, mostly pedro, for part of the evening and then square-danced into the night. Old and young danced together. Clyde Lyke, a neighbor and good friend of the family, loved to tease all of us kids and it was fun when he would be our partner in cards or in dancing. Clyde could pick up almost any stringed instrument and make it sound great. We were always impressed when he would get his jackknife out and slide it up and down the frets on the neck of his guitar, making it sound like a steel guitar.

Mom found time to read during the winter. Her favorite author went by the pen name of Gene Stratton-Porter. Porter's first name was actually Geneva, but her editor insisted she use the name "Gene" because it was assumed that books would sell better if written by a male author. Gene Stratton-Porter centered her novels on the outdoor world near her home in Indiana. One of her best-known books was *Girl of the Limberlost*, a story of a young girl's moth collections and the insect life in the Wabash County Limberlost Swamp. Dad spent more time in the house during the winter days, even taking time to read western novels by Zane Grey such as *Riders of the Purple Sage* and *Heritage of the Desert*.

CHAPTER 7 (1943)

ELECTRICITY, FIELD WORK, HERDING COWS

❧

The warm sun of spring could be felt when stepping outside that April day of 1943 as Cherryland Rural Electric wired our house. We had electricity! And, just as exciting, Dad built an indoor bathroom with a flush toilet in a corner of the laundry/junk room. Lights in the ceilings and electric lamps on the tables meant no more kerosene lamp chimneys to clean. Even the barn was wired, putting an end to the threat of accidentally starting a fire with the lighted lanterns hanging there every evening. Life was good!

Dad bought a new electric radio for better reception when listening to the evening news. Gabriel Heatter was his favorite newscaster. Heatter always began his broadcast with the words "There's g-o-o-d news tonight." His emphasis and drawl of the word "good" became a signature phrase to soften the harsh news of war. He especially liked to tell stories of bravery and heroic feats in the heat of battle. Dad sat with his ear almost glued to the radio and we did not disturb him during that half hour.

The Hit Parade was the radio program that I never wanted to miss as I reached twelve years old. All the latest popular songs were played with the #1 hit saved to the very last. One song that reached #1 might not have been described as very beautiful, but it was, well, different…Here are the lyrics: "Mairzy Doats and Dozy Doats and Liddle Lamzy Divey – A Kiddldey Divey, too, wouldn't you?" (To my grandchildren: yes, I could understand all the lyrics and sing right along with it. Have you figured out the translation yet?) When I searched for information about The Hit Parade, I was amazed to read that the hour-long program, geared to teenagers and young adults, was sponsored by American Tobacco Lucky Strike cigarettes with their slogan of "Reach for a Lucky instead of a sweet."

With our older brother now in the Navy, the spring of 1943 would bring other changes in addition to our electricity and indoor bathroom. Gene and I became Dad's hired hands. What a motley crew we were. We worked many long hours with him that first summer and for the next two consecutive seasons. I wonder, even yet, how he had the heart to continue raising crops with just the two of us to help.

A sixty-acre farm is not very large by today's standards, nor even as Dad worked his land. To create a self-sustaining farm operation on his sixty acres would depend on how he cared for the soil—that warm earth womb that nourishes and brings life to dried brown seeds and brittle kernels of corn. His harvest would depend on how he prepared the ground that beds fields of rye and strengthens the deep roots of alfalfa hay. Those fields would be the key to Dad's future. He was the architect, the designer. Out of necessity, he would become a veterinarian, weather forecaster, financial planner and fence mender. He would be governed by the work load rather than a clock or calendar. He would be pushed and pulled and limited and harried, threatened by approaching storms, dry spells, pests and weeds. There would be rainy seasons delaying planting time and early frosts hindering harvest time. But there would also be fields of tall golden wheat and potato patches where each hill produced enough spuds for a family meal and bean fields that would furnish our family with navy beans for bean soup on cold winter evenings or to make baked beans for the potluck meal before PTA meetings.

The notion that a corn crop should be knee high by the 4th of July prompts many farmers to get busy as soon as the weather warms in the spring. Preparing for planting the corn involved a number of different operations. Manure was spread on the field with a horse-pulled manure spreader. Then began the first of many farming tasks Gene and I would learn about. We rode together on a riding-plow pulled by a team of three horses and worked the field. Mom came out to snap a photo of us when we were ready to start the first furrow.

Gene and Virgina ready to begin plowing

Without that photo, I am not sure others would have believed someone as young as we were had the capability, or the courage, of assuming such a demanding task. Even now it sounds to me as if I might be imagining it, but we did ride that plow! Dad had explained that after we had made one round it would be necessary to have one horse walk in the just-plowed furrow to keep the future furrows straight. After we finished with the plowing, a horse-drawn heavy metal roller was pulled over the lumpy ground, breaking down the now-pliant soil. One final preparation involved a harrow—sometimes referred to as a drag—with iron claws which disturbed the soil just enough that the trail of a marking chain could be distinguished. At this point, four separate horse-drawn operations had been implemented.

Manual labor was needed to mark the corn rows and plant the seed; each of these processes also covered the entire field again. The row marker was made of a straight, slender pole with four or five chains fastened to it approximately one yard apart. The chains were heavy enough to leave a mark on the ground when carrying the pole across the field. Dad held up one end of the marking pole and Gene and I took turns holding the opposite end. It was a challenge to keep in stride with Dad. Our success, or failure, would be evident when the corn grew. The rows might be straight or there might be a few little curves betraying the places where we fell behind. From east to west and then north to south we walked holding those poles up, providing crossmarks to guide Dad. Using a hand corn planter, two or three kernels of corn were planted at each mark. The field was then weeded twice by a horse-drawn cultivator when the new corn shoots appeared. At harvest time, Dad cut the cornstalks, gathered them in large sheaves bundled with rope, stood them up, and left them to dry before shucking off the ears of corn. The dried stalks were used for cattle feed throughout the winter. In addition, Dad saved seed from those ears of corn to plant the following year.

Twelve times that field was worked over in the span of May through October—seven times by horses and driver, twice by Dad and Gene and me walking it with the row marker, once by Dad alone as he planted each hill, plus a couple rounds of cultivating when the corn plants were green and tender. But those hours spent working in the seven-acre corn field were just an accepted part of the total farming process; no hourly wage would be computed nor considered a component in the success or failure of a crop in this living-off-the-land lifestyle. Only the end result mattered. A good crop of corn rated high, a scant harvest rated low. After the corn was planted, we began the field preparation for potatoes and navy beans. In retrospect, Dad must have spent many hours calculating the crops needed even before we turned the first furrow. His expectation must have been that there would be a harvest sufficient to feed his family, his animals and have a surplus to sell for profit. A time of butchering took place after all the crops were in and that also must have been included in his planned end results at the close of the year. Hard work, vision and perseverance. Dad had those attributes, but they were little acknowledged or recognized. He was just a farmer making a living for his family.

One of my least favorite chores was milking cows. I did not ever enjoy this chore. It seemed like the only cow that would stand still and not switch her tail in my face was Old Beauty, a gentle Guernsey cow, so gentle that Gene and I sometimes rode around the barnyard on her back.

Cows are animals of habit. When we put them in the barn for milking, each would return to their same stanchion. When going to a familiar field for the day, they always turned in at the pasture gate with no herding. Gene tells of bringing them from the south pasture up the long lane to the barn. Taffy, one of Old Beauty's offspring, always walked close to one of the corner posts. If Gene ran ahead of her and climbed up that fence post, he could hop on her back and ride the rest of the way to the barn. Taffy never varied her habit of veering over near that fence post.

After school ended for the summer, it became my task, along with Cubbie, our collie dog, to herd our seven cows to pasture about a mile down the two-track road east of our farm. I was twelve years old and loved walking along behind the cattle, barefooted and carefree in the morning. Old Beauty always wore the cowbell and it sounded kind of musical to me, sort of a rhythmic ding-dong as she ambled along. The cattle all knew the way and needed little herding. I didn't have to watch for traffic on the sandy trail most mornings, just a neighbor occasionally heading for his nearby pasture. The daily trek wound through woods for a little space and sometimes I explored that area on my way home, looking for wildflowers or birds. The only house I would walk past was a deserted one that had belonged to a conservation officer. Broken windows, shingles blown off the roof, just in general disrepair. I always imagined there would be treasures in the house or the yard, and sometimes ignored the No Trespassing sign and explored a little but never found anything except some old bottles and rusty cans. The Ann Arbor railroad track ran alongside the pasture, but there were no other signs of habitation along the whole distance to that area, which we referred to as "back east."

One day for some reason I was a little late getting the herd on the trail to the pasture, which seemed to be no problem until we were nearing the railroad tracks and I heard a train whistle. The Ann Arbor passenger train was down around the bend coming our way. Most of the herd was already across the tracks when the engine came in sight, but Old Beauty, the pokey one, was just stepping over them. And, of all times, she caught her hoof between the crossing boards that allowed cars to drive over the tracks. Her hoof was wedged between the board and the steel track and though she was trying very hard to loosen it, she couldn't. Cubbie and I stood there helplessly watching as that black monstrous engine approached. The engineer had applied his brakes, but a train doesn't stop as easily as a car. Steam locomotives at that time had heavy metal bars shaped like a snowplow blade mounted to the front lower section of the engine, often called cowcatchers, for pushing objects off the tracks. The locomotive was getting mighty close when, in a panicky, desperate tug, Old Beauty freed her hoof and was off the tracks. It seemed like a scene from an old movie. Beauty started running, turned in at the pasture gate and kept running until she disappeared behind a small hill, her cowbell jangling wildly all the way. The engineer looked my way, wiped his brow with his red kerchief and waved. I was one frightened young girl. When I told my dad about it later, he listened, was glad to hear how it turned out, but I still had to herd those cows back and forth every day.

One of those same beautiful spring mornings as I came back from taking the cows to pasture, Dad was ready to mark the rows and begin planting our annual vegetable garden. This marking pole was smaller than the one we used in the corn field, usually a small branch from a sapling tree. I learned later that lots of gardeners used a string stretched out between two stakes in the ground to mark their rows. That sounded much easier to me, but probably seemed too slow for Dad. There was too much work to be done on the rest of the farm to fuss with string and stakes. Just three swings up and down the length of the garden with that wide marking pole dragging its chains and every row was marked out wide enough for a garden cultivator.

Gene and I soon learned how deep to plant each variety of seed and how to space them, knowledge that I used many, many times in the years ahead. For instance, radish seeds are tiny and the vegetable itself is very close to the surface when ready to be harvested, so there needs to be just a sprinkling of soil spread over the seed. I learned to transplant tomato and strawberry plants without disturbing the soil around their roots.

Soon the first crop of leaf lettuce would appear; next radishes were large enough to pull up, and peas and string beans hung from their vines. Later in the summer we would have juicy red tomatoes, sweet yellow ears of corn, cucumbers and squash. We had a veritable gourmet salad ripening all summer long. By the first snowfall, all the produce would be gathered, stored or canned, except for the parsnips. Their flavor seems to improve in the colder weather. How can a gardener describe the satisfaction of brushing winter's snow aside to pull the last fresh vegetable from the year's garden?

Gladiolas were Dad's favorite flower, but he always planted dahlias and marigolds, too. He often picked a few gladiolas after he was through working in the garden in the evening. Dad's organic gardening methods were simple. No commercial fertilizer or spray— he had an easy and more cost-effective way to rid the plants of pests. That easy method was to send Gene and me out to the garden to pick potato bugs off the early potato plants and exterminate them by dropping them into a little jar of kerosene. Tomato plants were another story. I refused to touch those fat green worms that eat the leaves and chew on the little green tomatoes. Gene had to pick them off.

Mom often saved and dried tomato seeds from tomatoes we had grown in the garden. In early March of the following year, she filled containers with dirt, planted the seeds, watered and kept them where the sun would shine on them. That is one more example of the many ways my parents utilized what they had; also, it is a small example of sustainable farming, though I suspect Mom saved those seeds because it was a brand they liked, not necessarily to preserve heirloom tomatoes.

We constantly recycled to save money. Environmental concerns happened naturally. No garbage truck stopped by to pick up our trash. We threw scrap foods to the chickens and what little waste paper we had we burned in a barrel and dumped the trash barrel contents in a ravine of one of the fields. Mom saved small brown paper bags for our school lunches, as well as any scrap of paper that could be used for a grocery list and old newspapers for starting fires in the morning. When our clothes were worn out, she cut them into scraps for quilts, rags, or patches. White cotton material was cut into strips and saved to use as bandages. No plastic containers existed until the 1940's and early 1950's. There were never any patios, decks, or other artificial coverings in our yard or the barnyard, just grass, gravel and dirt. We shoveled our driveway out by hand when it snowed. Dad used no commercial fertilizer in the fields, at least in the early years, just old-fashioned barn manure.

In my memory, the three hardest tasks every year—and most dreaded in hot weather—were picking up stones in the potato field before planting began, picking cucumbers when they reached the marketable size, and harvesting hay.

Stones were everywhere in the potato patch. Some

of the stones were the size of eggs and others as large as a soccer ball. Dad fashioned a crude stone boat with a flat board rack attached to small logs for skids, then hitched it to his snorting, breathing, live horse-power. We tossed the rocks onto the stone boat and dumped them in a nearby washed-out ravine, Dad's version of a landfill. But the next year, there were just as many stones in the same field as there had been the previous year. One more year of picking up stones, I thought, would be the year I began searching seed catalogs for actual stone seeds. There must be a propagation going on—how else could there be this many every year? Dad's seed potatoes came from last year's crop. By planting time, they were shriveled and looked as if they should have been thrown away. But if we cut them properly, making sure there was an "eye" (potential sprout) in each piece, each chunk of tuber would grow and produce a fine new crop of potatoes.

We often saw killdeer birds when working in the field. They make their nests on the ground in open fields where the grass is short and there are no bushes nearby. Of course, our presence was alarming to them. It was a bit comical to watch the male killdeer begin his ruse of distraction by hobbling and flapping one wing as if he were hurt, hoping to draw the intruding worker away from the nest and toward him. We kept a careful watch for the nest to avoid disturbing it.

"It's time to pick pickles." Those words usually produced a big groan. They were an important cash crop, but I have no fond recollections of those days, only memories of an aching back from bending over those vines sprawled along the ground in the hot sun. Cucumbers needed to be harvested at the right size, about one or two inches in diameter and five inches long, to bring the best price when taken to the Mesick pickle station. My cousin Dulce, who lived near Flint, spent two or three weeks with us for a few summers. She always helped with whatever job we were given, including the cucumber picking. I think she even enjoyed it. She always wanted to stay a little longer when her folks drove up to get her. What could attract a girl who lived in the city to enjoy farm work? I could never quite believe that she really liked to pick pickles.

No automated hay baler rolling up round bales of hay ever operated in the Mack hay field when my brother and I were the field hands. Just the two of us and our dad harvested and stacked it in the barn, high in the hay mow. Harvesting hay is a dicey business. The ripe stalks are mowed and raked into windrows, forked over once to dry the underside, and loaded and hauled into the barn. If harvested at the right stage and no rain falls on the cut hay, it will be of high quality for the animals. If it rains on hay that has been cut, the hay will not be of the same quality when dried and stored. But there is one more challenge: the hay needs to be completely dry before it is heaped in the hay loft to avoid the danger of combustion. Fortunately, no barn fires occurred in the loft during the years we lived there.

When the hay was dry enough, Dad pitched it onto a large wooden wagon with eight-feet-tall racks attached to the front and back. One of us arranged the hay with a pitchfork to keep the load level and the other one drove the horses. That was hard, dusty, and sweaty work. Getting the hay up into the haymow was also stressful. When the loaded wagon was situated near the high loft in the barn a large iron two-pronged forklift thrust deep into the hay clutched a hay bunch with its forked prongs, and pulled the hay up into the mow using a horse-drawn pulley. The hay was released, the fork brought back down and loaded with another cluster of hay.

We knew threshing season loomed ahead when fields of wheat turned golden in the area. Dad always had at least one crop of grain, alternating between oats and wheat, or sometimes fields of both. The scheduled day to thresh at our farm caused a flurry of preparation. The wheat crop was cut and bundled and loaded on wagons. Mom had extra help to prepare a hearty noon meal of mashed potatoes and gravy and platters of roast beef, homemade bread or biscuits, and pies. The crew generally consisted of at least six men. Have you ever heard the term "enough here to feed threshers" when sitting down to a huge Thanksgiving meal? After watching the threshing crew empty a dish of mashed potatoes and scoop out a second heaping bowlful while talking and joking and discussing their crops, I could identify with the phrase. When the dinner bell rang, the men, their

Mom's brothers harvesting hay

faces grimy and coveralls thick with chaff dust, rinsed their hands and face in a large galvanized tub filled with water set just outside the kitchen door. I always went across the road to help Leona Robinson prepare dinner for the threshers at their farm.

Threshing day started early with the lumbering, awkward-looking gray metal threshing machine arriving to set up its steam engine and pulleys; the machines resembled a huge bucket of metal riveted together in haphazard style—a pulley here and little wheels there, chutes raised up skyward for blowing chaff away, other chutes with gunny sacks fastened to catch the grain. By the end of the day, granary bins were filled and the machine headed for another farm. It was truly a neighborhood event!

Fresh cut hay carries a delightful clean fragrance for months after it is harvested. Candles and colognes in a number of specialty boutiques now carry that scent, even listing it as "Fresh Hay" in some shops. It's possible that the Walter T. Rawleigh Company missed an opportunity to make a fortune when peddling their wares in rural America in the thirties and forties. Wouldn't every young housewife and/or her daughter want a bottle of this fine country fragrance on their dresser? The Rawleigh salesman sold spices and vanilla and pepper in large containers, along with many other products, including some cosmetics, but no Fresh Hay colognes. They carried salves for the family medicine chest and a number of medicinal salves for animals, as well. I remember the Fuller Brush salesman showing his wares for personal, household and animal needs such as hair brushes, cleaning brushes and curry brushes for horses. Because the products were dependable, most people welcomed the knock on their door as their favorite traveling salesman worked his route. It was a convenience of importance in the busy farm life.

In addition to the friendly visits of traveling salesmen, we could look forward to the county bookmobile turning into our driveway during summer months. Imagine a bus full of books for all the family to choose from coming right to our house, books such as the Nancy Drew series, the Boxcar Children and the Hardy Boys mysteries for Gene and me, along with a large selection of non-fiction and novels of interest to Mom and Dad. This lending library provided reading opportunities for rural families who seldom, if ever, visited a library because the nearest one might be twenty or thirty miles away.

Our telephone was pure country, of course, an eight-party line in which a neighbor could listen to your conversation by quietly lifting their receiver off the hook. In addition, the phones were generally attached to a wall and a teenager could not take the phone to his/her room for a little privacy. Each customer on the phone line had an assigned ring, such as two short rings and one long one. Long distance calls were made by ringing up the operator in Mesick who would connect you with your party.

The hard days of work for Dad and us kids that summer went by with no problems getting the crops in, but by Saturday afternoons, we were ready to take a break. Dad liked to go to the free shows on Saturday night and he didn't work on Sunday, except morning and evening chores. Marjorie sometimes came home on weekends and quite often, on a Sunday afternoon, neighborhood kids and cousins walked or rode their bikes (the one-speed kind with tube tires) to our house for a game of softball.

In our softball games, the ash tree served as first base, a rock marked second base and a nearby apple tree was third. The garage wall and the person at bat acted as catcher. That same wall had a window in it made of unbreakable Plexiglas taken from a Model T Ford (another of Dad's money-savers), so we didn't have to worry about hitting it with a wild pitch and breaking it. Sometimes we set up a croquet game, the kind often seen played on immaculate manicured lawns of the socially elite. The wire arches were sunk into hard sod between the ash tree and two apple trees with the thorn hedge at one end and our garage at the other. Our yard was level only because it "grew" that way. It received no thatching, no new sod and was raked only once in early spring, but what competitive fun we had, untended lawn and all. Quack grass often grew tall enough to resemble a hay field. Lilac bushes and pink wild roses prospered untended in the backyard, their stubborn roots pushing up through thick tangles of grass. The delicate little rose petals bloomed each spring bearing a sweet romantic fragrance—a pearl among the pile of wood chips thrown casually nearby. Even some hardy asparagus spears, uncultivated, pushed up through the sod in early spring.

Mom usually made homemade ice cream to serve after the games, using real cream from the farm and, as an egg substitute, she added junket tablets for thickening which gave it more flavor. When the hand-cranked freezer could no longer be turned indicating the ice cream was hard, everyone scooped out a bowlful and made sure to thank Mom for the perfect ending of an afternoon of fun.

CHAPTER 8 (1943-1945)

RATIONING, KAPOK, VICTORY GARDENS

By July 1943, Dean was on a ship and his letters were censored, so we didn't know where he was, but he wrote regularly and my parents welcomed those letters. As the war progressed on both fronts, wartime needs prompted the distribution of books of ration stamps to each household member. Stamps had to accompany each purchase of canned fruits and vegetables, fats and vegetable oils, butter, sugar, shoes, tires, gasoline, coal, fuel oil, and a number of other items. So stringent were the restrictions that, when applying for ration books, women were requested to report the amount of sugar they already had stored in their cabinet. Stamps equal to that amount were immediately removed from their new ration book. The Sears & Roebuck catalog cautioned customers to be sure they included the necessary ration stamps when ordering shoes.

An example of the rigorous system involved in using these stamps is seen in this notice published in

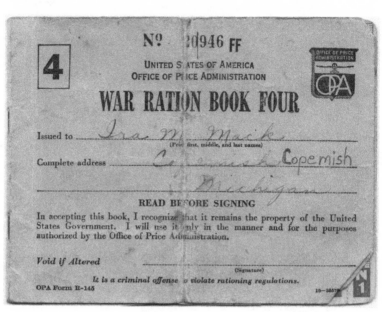

Ira's war ration book

the July 31, 1943 issue of the *Cadillac Evening News:* "Processed Foods: Blue stamps, N, P, and Q good thru August 7. Sugar: Stamp 13 good for 5 lbs. thru August 15 and stamps 15, 16 each good for five pounds of canning sugar between now and October 1. Meats, cheese, butter: Red Stamp P,Q,R,S valid now, expires July 31. T valid now thru August. Shoes: #18 good now thru October 31." Restrictive consumer guidelines such as these would stay in effect until after the war ended.

The government began urging everyone to cultivate a Victory Garden and grow their own vegetables to ensure adequate food for the troops. Green beans and peas and other easy-to-grow vegetables sprouted up in boxes of soil on city rooftops. In addition to the rooftop gardens, potted tomato vines were seen on patios and back porches. Students from kindergarten to high school planted vegetable gardens in schoolyards which later appeared on their lunch trays. Window boxes of greens appeared in the homes of elderly people who were unable to work in gardens, but wanted to join in the cause. Victory Gardens brought a new purpose to kitchens for women who had never before preserved vegetables and fruits as they began to can and freeze their garden produce. Young women could attend classes to learn the skill of canning. In my family, we just continued to preserve our home-grown vegetables as usual. We did not experience the shortage of many foods during rationing, because of our large garden.

In addition to Victory Gardens, demands for goods were springing up in other areas. Kapok, the material which provided buoyancy for lifejackets, was no longer available; formerly purchased from the nation of Indonesia where kapok trees flourish, that supply chain was now under Japanese occupation. The shortage of lifejackets became critical in all branches of the service. A search for substitute buoyant material began. Various experiments with cork, cattail down, feathers and a plastic bubble were tried but none seemed a satisfactory replacement until, finally, a surprising and unexpected source was discovered. Boris Berkman, a Chicago physician, had long thought the common milkweed had possibilities for various uses and one day in his research he noted that the floss in each pod, the silky white hairs fastened to each seed, were hollow and coated with a natural wax. After testing, they were found to be adequate for providing buoyancy to the life-jackets.

This began a most interesting campaign involving young people anxious to help in the war effort and eager to show their patriotism and concern for service men and women. Northern Michigan was found to have one of the largest milkweed concentrations of the common milkweed, *Asclerpias syriaca*, in the nation, and consequently, was in the forefront of producing buoyant fiber fillers for the armed services. The Navy set an overall goal of obtaining 300,000 pounds of floss before the war's end, which meant harvesting two million pounds of milkweed pods. Distribution centers handed out orange onion bags to fill. Each bagful was worth fifteen cents. The pods had to be picked at the right stage of maturity—ripe, but not split open. The initial drive to harvest them occurred in September and October of 1943 and again the following year. Clusters of three or four pods hung together with two or three clusters on each mature stalk of the milkweed plant. They were very easy to gather. School children all over the area, including Gene and I, combed fallow fields for the egg-shaped, rough, warty pods. (Incidentally, the milkweed is in demand once again but for quite a different reason. The monarch butterfly depends almost totally on the milkweed as its primary source of nourishment, and

Over-ripe pods burst open with silky floss spilling out.
Milkweed pods unopened at left and bottom.

consequently the butterfly population has declined. Local garden shops now carry packets of milkweed seeds for sale along with other garden seeds. Gardeners and landscapers are encouraged to plant a few milkweeds in among their flowers and shrubs and vegetable rows to attract butterflies. Also, a milkweed cluster of pods, with a bit of floss bursting from one, can add a certain charm to a fall bouquet of flowers.)

Victory gardens, gas rationing, scrap metal drives and milkweed pods! By autumn of 1943, the intensity of the war seemed to permeate every facet of life whether you lived on a sparsely-populated gravel road in rural Michigan or in the heart of New York City or Los Angeles. Farmers were required to sign a form certifying the number of tires they had on their property, allowing one spare tire for a car. Any scrap tires had to be sold to the U.S. Government as scrap rubber for twenty cents a tire. Dad had two extra tires. He could choose to be paid by check, in Defense Stamps or donate to the Defense Supplies. He chose to receive a check for the forty cents. Forty cents? A postage stamp costs more than that now. But with lightweight long-legged underwear selling for $1.25 per pair, six scrap tires could outfit a farmer for the winter.

Drivers were constantly reminded on billboards, on government forms and by radio to "Obey 35 mph speed limits, stop slowly, start slowly and turn slowly to save wear on tires." The slogan "Is this trip really necessary?" appeared everywhere. Also, during the war, it was a common sight to see frustrated drivers parked alongside the road with a jack hoisting up their car bumper as they changed or repaired a tire. Tube repair kits were carried in most glove compartments in anticipation of flat tires, since the rubber tubes weakened with wear and were usually patched and used again. Dad also had to account for the mileage on his 1934 Chevrolet sedan, according to two forms found in his file dated November 1944 and June 1945. Slogans assured citizens that these efforts would help save lives on the battlefield and our soldiers would have the equipment and food and clothing they needed.

Junk from Farms

and its place in the War

Back of the barn, in the tool shed, out in the orchard and down in the gully is a lot of Junk which is doing no good where it is, but which is needed at once to help smash the Japs and Nazis.

Scrap iron and steel, for example.

Even in peacetime, scrap provided about 50% of the raw material for steel. It may be rusty, old "scrap" to you, but it is actually *refined* steel — with most impurities removed, and can be quickly melted with new metal in the form of pig iron to produce highest quality steel for our war machines.

The production of steel has gone *up, up,* **UP,** until today America is turning out as much steel as all the rest of the world combined. But unless at least 6,000,000 additional tons of scrap steel is uncovered promptly, the full rate of production cannot be attained or increased; all the tanks, guns and ships our country is counting on cannot be produced.

The rubber situation is also critical. In spite of the recent rubber drive, there is a continu-

ing need for large quantities of scrap rubber. Also for other waste materials and metals like brass, copper, zinc, lead and tin. The need is urgent.

The Junk which you collect is bought by industry from scrap dealers at established, government-controlled prices.

* * *

Will you help?

Will you scour every fence corner on your farm and get your Junk into circulation?

First—collect it and pile it up.

Then, if there is no Junk dealer in your vicinity who will come and get it, get in touch with your County War Board or your farm implement dealer. In many communities a "Scrap Harvest" is being planned. Co-operate in this and get your neighbors to cooperate.

Throw YOUR scrap into the fight!

JUNK MAKES FIGHTING WEAPONS

One old disc will provide scrap steel needed for 210 semi-automatic light carbines.

One old plow will help make one hundred 15-mm. armor-piercing projectiles.

One useless old tire provides as much rubber as is used in 12 gas masks.

One old shovel will help make 4 hand grenades.

MATERIALS NEEDED

Scrap iron and steel,

Other metals of all kinds,

Old rubber, rags, Manila rope, burlap bags.

Waste cooking fats—When you get a pound or more, strain into a big tin can and sell to your meat dealer.

NEEDED ONLY IN CERTAIN AREAS—Waste paper and tin cans, as announced locally.

NOT NEEDED (at this time)—Razor blades—glass.

This message approved by Conservation Division **WAR PRODUCTION BOARD** This advertisement paid for by the American Industries Salvage Committee (representing and with funds provided by a group of leading industrial concerns).

Farm magazine ad during WW2

"Do less so they have enough," and, "If you don't need it, DON'T BUY IT!"

Even women who sewed their own clothes had certain guidelines regarding the size of belts (only two inches wide) and no cuffs on the sleeves of dresses, blouses and shirts, since textile manufacturers were faced with creating uniforms for the military even as fabric supplies dwindled. Once again blouses and dresses were fashioned using grain feed sacks, just as they had during the years of the Depression. Very few women or girls wore slacks. Housekeeping ads were still featuring the woman of the house with heels on and a nice dress with a frilly apron whether she was cooking breakfast or doing the laundry. However, during the war, women who worked in factories began to wear work pants on the job. The fictitious character Rosie the Riveter's "We Can Do It" posters were plastered everywhere. She became an icon with her bandana and bulging arm muscles, implying that women could do the work of men when needed. This encouraged the fashion world and a 1943 issue of *Modern Screen* magazine featured actresses Marlene Dietrich and Kathryn Hepburn with their newest pant styles. But Mom never chose to wear slacks. By the time I was in high school, girls were seen in school photos with slacks on, but even then, we still primarily wore dresses.

It seemed each winter that Mom's accumulated pile of mending was as big as the year before. Men generally wore wool socks in the winter. Their buckle overshoes often leaked and caused holes in the socks, but wool socks were expensive footwear and in short supply, so Mom repaired them with some yarn and a knitting needle. She sewed dresses for herself, shirts for Gene and blouses for me. She also found time to enjoy her pastime of tatting and embroidering. Tatting consisted of a metal shuttle about four inches long with thread wound on a spool inside and, when used properly, created knots and circles that were joined together in patterns to form doilies, decorative lace trim for collars, and edgings of pillowcases. Tatting became a lost art over the years—women no longer wore tatted lace collars on their dresses and doilies were no longer popular. However, tatting patterns have appeared once again in crochet-themed magazines.

Mom and I put many Walt Whitman Guild jigsaw puzzles together every winter. Whitman began selling puzzles in 1923 but in the Forties when we worked on them, we agreed that the company had not improved their product much in the two decades since they were first marketed. Pieces still did not interlock firmly. If we jarred the table or pushed something against the side of the puzzle, the pieces dislodged and we would have to refit them. I am still an avid puzzle fan, but I appreciate the newer puzzles with pieces that interlock in a secure fashion. Anagrams, a word game similar to Scrabble, was a popular pastime in the world of games at that time, and I thoroughly enjoyed competing with Mom using our word skills. Our family loved to play games. Most men really enjoyed carroms, a game similar to pool, but on a much smaller scale. Chinese checkers, a marble game with colorful dragons and paper lanterns decorating the playing board, became very popular, too.

During the winter of 1944-1945, Dad took some time to teach me how to hang wallpaper. It was kind of an apprenticeship, though I suspect his real reason was because he needed a helper. But I did enjoy learning the art of paper hanging. For example, I learned that in older houses one of the surest areas to begin securing it was on the right side of an exterior door, since most doors were constructed to open and shut easily and generally were built with straight lines. If the paper could be hung absolutely straight up and down there, then the rest of the room would be the same (with adept paper hangers). I liked that work and in later years did some decorative papering in some of the houses we owned.

I learned to stack wood after Dad had cut it into the right lengths for our stove. I enjoyed stacking wood, too, if it wasn't blowing and snowing and too cold. Care needs to be taken in placing chunks of wood on top of one another to keep the pile straight and fitted together so it doesn't fall over.

Warm days and cold nights in February or March of each year brought on the season of tapping maple trees. After two or three holes were drilled in a tree, a spile was inserted in each hole for the sap to course down into a hanging bucket. At times, Dad supplemented his supply of metal spiles by using short sections of branches from the sumac bushes that grew randomly around the farm. Sumac branches have a soft inner section that can be hollowed out and they worked fine when needed. The production of maple syrup was a very time-consuming task at that time. Modern equipment now has stream-lined the gathering process. Approximately forty gallons of sap is needed to produce one gallon of thick, sweet maple syrup. When the buckets hanging on the trees were full we poured them into barrels on the sleigh and from there into a large black iron kettle hung over a fire pit. Family members tended the fire late into the night, adding wood when necessary. When a certain thickness was reached, the syrup was taken into the kitchen and boiled down to the consistency that pours so easily over a hot stack of pancakes.

One winter, perhaps it was in 1945, though I cannot be certain of that, I experienced an especially beautiful and quiet evening solitude. It was the kind of day in March when frosty cold weather struggles to stay around just a few more days and the warming sun is teasing it to leave. Late in the evening my brother Gene and I decided to see if the melting snow that day had formed a pond in our neighbor's field and if it had now frozen enough to skate on. We picked up our snap-on skates and told our parents where we were going. Stepping out into the crisp night even the unpainted barn buildings seemed to be suspended in moon glow, the barn roof silhouetted across the sky. No beaming headlights or shining yard lights, no droning airplane overhead, just an empty field with a pond frozen so clear a reflection from the moon hung over it. Sparkling stars now covered the sky like salt pouring out of a shaker. Clipping on our skates, we stumbled a bit, then got our bearings and skated back and forth across the little pond, sometimes slowly, sometimes seeing how fast we could go.

As we finished skating and began walking back to our yard, I could see the hedge, that pesky one with prickly thorns, outlined in the moonlight and shining snow. It was as if an artist had transformed its gnarly branches into a protecting shield around our yard, letting us know all was well and we were safe. I was a country girl surrounded by riches.

CHAPTER 9 (1945-1960)

War Over, Seeds, Sale of Farm

What a relief it was on May 8, 1945, when the radio station interrupted its usual program to announce that Germany had surrendered and fighting had ceased on the European continent. In August, Japan surrendered. WWII was over. But in the aftermath of the atomic bomb advent, mankind now for the first time would be forced to reckon with the knowledge that a weapon capable of wreaking untold destruction and suffering existed.

In Europe, nations that had been decimated with bombs and battle-scarred land sought humanitarian relief. Plagued with food shortages, farmers in the war-torn regions found themselves without farm equipment, and most importantly, without seeds. Over four hundred thousand acres of agricultural land had been destroyed along with root plants. Starvation loomed. The United Nations Relief and Rehabilitation Administration (UNRRA) had a staff member, Ethel Pattison, who had spent years working with seeds, developing new hardier varieties, providing information to farmers in countries around the world. Pattison, who over the years had earned a reputation as the seed lady, was called upon to help alleviate the problem. Thanks to her visionary nature, she foresaw that there would be a need for seeds in huge quantities when peace returned to the European continent. The United Nations commissioned her to determine the seeds needed most in each nation and how to get them there. Mrs. Pattison wheedled hundreds of tons of seeds from nations with abundant supplies, though some were not anxious to share. Italy needed seed potatoes, field peas and spring vetch. Czechoslovakia (now divided into two nations) had a severe shortage of alfalfa seeds, as well as spring wheat and buckwheat. Other nations needing help were Greece, the Ukraine and Austria. This was a humanitarian effort on a scale never before experienced among so many nations. A woman with a passion for tiny seeds had set out to bring healing to those who had suffered and lost so much. In her humble fashion, Mrs. Pattison brought beauty to the ugly, scarred landscape and hope to masses of needy people. She was truly an artist of the highest order. She said in an interview published in the May 1946 *Farm Journal*, "Farm women must dream and dream straight. Their fields and forests are an entire world, a universe of their very own. Think of something so common as a small, dull seed. Such a tiny thing is my world, but it is limitless."

After reading about Mrs. Pattison, I became curious about how many seeds there were in a melon I had just cut open. I counted over six hundred. My mind could not fathom how many cantaloupes could be raised from just that one little round fruit I held in my hand. If each seed would produce one vine, the melon I had cut open could produce six hundred new plants and melons ad infinitum. I was impacted by the thought of how vital farms are in the efforts to alleviate world hunger.

The spring of 1946 would be the final summer for Dad's two farm hands to be called upon for long days of farm labor. Dean was home from the Navy and

1943 Back: Dad, Mom, Dean. Front: Virginia, Gene, Marjorie.

the rhythm of Dad's farming was changing, as well. Dad had a cooling shed for the whole milk he sold, and bought a tractor to ease his work in the fields. He was farming much less land. The corn shocks that used to be left out in the field into the winter months now were shredded and filled the new silo erected at one end of the barn. Known as sileage, the new method of harvesting corn was fast, economical and good for the cattle. As a result, another icon from the past disappeared; those picturesque scenes of dried bundled corn stalks with snow blanketing the ground around them would no longer be available for photographers or artists.

Soon, we learned that Uncle Mike would not be celebrating New Year's Eve with us. He had taken a job on a dairy farm in North Carolina. And now Alvina would be leaving. I was sure I would never see her again. Years later, thanks to the marvel of air travel, she and I spent many hours together getting re-acquainted as we filled in the gaps of her life in New York City and mine raising a family not all that many miles away from where we learned our ABC's together.

My teenage world just kept a-changin'—it was about that same time that I first heard of the cars that didn't require a clutch to shift gears. How could a car keep from stalling without a clutch? But our next-door neighbor, Clarence Robinson, bought one and I rode in it. It was true. Just step on the brake and the car would idle, not stall.

In October of that year, Dad, who now could relax from the pressures of long days in the field, challenged me one autumn evening to some target practicing. The days were getting chillier and thoughts of hunting season and white-tailed deer laced the conversation of men (and even a few women). Hunters set up their deer blinds. They cleaned their guns and hauled out their straw-filled bullseye targets for practice. And so, this day I followed Dad out to the apple orchard and laughed a little when I saw the target. No straw here, just a tobacco tin setting on a fencepost. Dad's thrifty nature evident once again! We were going to aim at a 3"x 6" tin tobacco can—the red one with Prince Albert posed in the large oval center. I had tried shooting squirrels once or twice, never coming close to them, and had very little experience with a gun. But this day, I lifted the .22 rifle, took aim, fired and placed the bullet right in the oval center of the tin. Dad decided I should have a deer license for the season. Uncle Frank, Dad's younger brother, would be hunting with us. Frank always came a day or so before the season opened carrying bags of bacon, eggs, homemade bread, lunch meat, store-bought cookies, a bag of Eight-O-Clock coffee from A&P, and nuts and candy. That in itself was pretty exciting!

Traditional hunting gear at that time included heavy red wool plaid shirts and pants with matching hat. November arrived and I suppose I must have had something red on (but no red plaid shirt), and I was sitting on a stump at the edge of a woods about two miles from the farm. I was so bundled up I could hardly walk, but I was warm. The rest of the hunting party knew that I was assigned to sit across the narrow two-track road from the big pine tree, a monolith that hunters used over the years to orient their hunting spots. That tree should have had a plaque hung on it, designating it as a centering tree for deer hunters. I don't think I even caught a glimpse of a deer during the whole season, but I can still feel the quiet of sitting in the woods when the snow is thick on the ground, hardwood trees are bare of leaves, fir trees are fragrant and nothing is moving, not a person in sight. No voices, no traffic, no dogs barking, just silence. Cold, crisp air and silence. And trees.

Trees provide a unique quality of restfulness, of strength and stability just by their very presence. Maple trees have wonderful qualities. Their beauty in the autumn season is breathtaking. Entering a small woodlot of maple trees on a sunny day, it's as if you stepped inside an oil painting that came to life with a swirl of fragrant rustling leaves. Their wood product when harvested creates furniture of the finest grained finish. Even a decaying maple tree produces a board finish called spalting that is often sought after by craftsmen. Spalting occurs when fungus invades the dying tree. Its decay forms an intricate ink-flow design, which brings out a beautiful grain pattern if sawn and polished by a knowledgeable woodworker. Maple logs for fireplaces produce a very warm heat and soothing crackling complete with sparks. When the seeds of a maple tree fall, the ground is covered for as far out as the branches extend. Each seed pod is a butterfly-shaped packet with at least six seeds in each one. Thousands and thousands of seeds from each tree each season. A potential forest could evolve from just one generous maple tree.

In 1949, Mom experienced what must have been a highlight of her life. She and a niece, Lucille, traveled to Oregon by train so Mom could visit her brother Herman and sister Bertha and their families, many of whom she had not seen for years.

That same summer, Dad and I occasionally filled the back of his brand new 1949 Chevrolet pickup truck with garden produce and flowers to peddle in Traverse City. We went first to Interlochen State Park, and I remember being amazed at how many of the tent campers bought a bouquet of flowers in addition to green beans and radishes and lettuce and tomatoes. Where would you display flowers in a tent? I guess the beauty of flowers brings a smile to the female population even in a tent, especially if that tent is surrounded by the fragrance and beauty of trees. Our next stop was Chum's gas station near Traverse City. The manager bought some gladiolas which he put on display for sale inside the station. Somewhere inside Dad, that quiet father of mine, innovative sales ideas must have been originating in his mind as he peddled his beloved flowers at state parks and gas stations.

To everything there is a season…Plans were made to sell the farm. Dad's final harvest on his sixty-acre farm had come to an end. Oh, there would still be things to keep him busy through the winter such as butchering-time and husking corn and sorting more of his navy beans, but all the crops were in—potatoes dug, ears of corn piled in the corn crib, granary bins filled with wheat and oats and beans, a hayloft stacked with hay. There would be no more poring over seed catalogs this winter or planning where to plant the corn next year.

In May of 1960, an auctioneer stood up on his auction block and, with neighbors standing nearby, began the bidding process. One by one, Taffy, an offspring of Old Beauty, our favorite Guernsey cow, plus the rest of the herd, were sold to the highest bidder. Pigs and hay wagons and harnesses came next. The seasonal rhythm of the farm would no longer govern Dad's days. His stubborn hope and determination had brought to fruition his dream of a debt-free farm, some savings in the local Mesick bank, his children grown and making lives of their own. Life in the Harlan community was at an end. Mom would no longer take her crates of eggs to sell at Wagner's store nor buy her groceries there. My parents moved into a small house near Interlochen, next door to my sister, Marjorie, and her family.

My image of a calm and steady non-adventurous father has changed a bit over the years. I am remembering traits and quirks, such as peddling gladiolas to a gas station manager, traits that were creating an enigma of the man who milked cows and cultivated corn. There was a day when some of his young grandchildren were visiting him at the little house in Interlochen where he and Mom lived after selling the farm—a day that I only learned about years later. He was telling the grandkids about some coins he had saved over the years. Then Dad stepped up on a kitchen chair, removed a piece of ceiling tile, reached up into the rafters and brought down a brown, shoebox-size leather case to show them his collection. He had a rapt audience—the grandkids were mesmerized with his hiding place, kind of like a Nancy Drew mystery. Along with the coins, Dad had kept the metal buttons from his uniform, the stripe of his promotion to Private First Class, postcards of the city of La Pallice where he was stationed in France, and the two letters from Mom. The brown leather case was put back, the ceiling tile returned to its spot, and no one saw the case again until after his death in 1978.

Dad managed to really surprise his adult children, as well, a few years after Mom passed away in 1966. He drove into his yard one day in a bright red Chevy Corvair, one of those sporty cars with bucket seats that has the engine in the back, located where the trunk is on most cars. It was his, bought and paid for. He had consulted none of us. We had no idea he was looking for a different car. How could we ever associate that snazzy little auto with the man who always bought practical cars? Who never bought one until the old one threatened to quit running? We still shake our heads.

But we're smiling as we remember Dad sitting in the driver's seat of his little red Corvair.

Dad had a garden for as long as he lived, albeit a much smaller one than on his farm. One day, long after he had retired, I walked with him down the rows of peas and green beans and gladiolas. He still wore bib overalls, but one thing had changed. He asked me to pick a few peas for him, saying he just couldn't bend over like that anymore. I recognized, then, that Marjorie's family had prepared the small plot for his garden and they also planted and hoed and harvested his vegetables. But it was still Dad's garden. He could walk among the rows each day and check to see how much the peas had grown and watch for the first little green tomato.

Soil grows strong roots. It produces taproots of hope and promise and sustenance of life. Ira knew that. He was a locavorist!

CPSIA information can be obtained
at www.ICGtesting.com
Printed in the USA
FSHW011701050519
57863FS